D0538532

It's My State!

MAINE

The Pine Tree State

Terry Allen Hicks, Amanda Hudson, and Van Kirk McCombs

Published in 2015 by Cavendish Square Publishing, LLC
243 5th Avenue, Suite 136, New York, NY 10016

First Edition

Library of Congress Cataloging-in-Publication Data

Hicks, Terry Allan.
Maine / Terry Allan Hicks, Amanda Hudson, Van Kirk McCombs. — Third edition.
pages cm. — (It's my state!)
Includes bibliographical references and index.
ISBN 978-1-50260-021-9 (library binding) ISBN 978-1-50260-022-6 (ebook)
1. Maine—Juvenile literature. I. Hudson, Amanda. II. McCombs, Van Kirk. III. Title.

F19.3.H53 2015
974.1—dc23

2014025539

Editor: Fletcher Doyle
Senior Copy Editor: Wendy A. Reynolds
Art Director: Jeffrey Talbot
Designer: Joseph Macri
Senior Production Manager: Jennifer Ryder-Talbot
Production Editor: David McNamara
Photo Research by J8 Media

The photographs in this book are used by permission and through the courtesy of: Cover photo by Ron and Patty Thomas Photography/E+/Getty Images; © Michelson, Robert S/Animals Animals, 4; Superstock: Thomas Kitchin &Vict/All Canada Photos, 4 (top); Minden Pictures, 4 (center); Muhammad Mahdi Karim/ File:Apis mellifera flying.jpg/Wikimedia Commons, 5; Alamy: Byron Jorjorina, 5 (right); F1 ONLINE, 5 (top); K.L. Kohn/Shutterstock.com, 6; Vernon Siql, 8; Hemis.fr, 11;Radius Images, 12; Michael P. Gadomski, 13;Israel Pabon/Shutterstock.com, 14; Portland Press Herald/Getty Images, 14; Jeffrey M. Frank/Shutterstock.com, 15; Colin D. Young/Shutterstock.com, 15; Cosmo Condina, 15 (center); Jerry and Marcy Monkman/EcoPhotography.com, 16; Erin Paul Donovan, 17; suefeldberg/iStock/ Thinkstock, 18; Danita Delimont, 18; James Urbach, 18 (top); PaulTessier/iStock/Thinkstock, 19; photos_martYmage/iStock/Thinkstock, 19; Tom Till, 19 (top); Brandon Cole Marine Photography, 20; Belinda Images, 21; Jeff Greenberg, 22; Giustino Menescardi/ File:JohnCabotPainting.jpg/ Wikimedia Commons, 24; EcoPhotography. com, 25; Ellen McKnight, 26; North Wind Picture Archives, 29; North Wind Picture Archives, 31; Lebrecht Music and Arts Photo Library, 33; Portland Press Herald/Getty Images, 34; Boston Globe/Getty Images, 34; E. Sweet/Shutterstock.com, 34; Portland Press Herald/Getty Images, 35; Daderot/File:Quad - Bowdoin College - IMG 7791. JPG/Wikimedia Commons, 35; Portland Press Herald/Getty Images, 35; Old Paper Studios, 37; Corbis: Bettmann, 38; David R. Frazier Photolibrary, Inc., 39; Unknown/ File:Log Pile of the Great Northern Paper Co., Millinocket, ME.jpg/Wikimedia Commons, 41; Rabbi Bob/Mike Beane/ File:ScottPaperMill WinslowMaine MikeBeane.jpg/ Wikimedia Commons, 42; BlueGreen Pictures, 44; Associated Press, 46;Visions of America, LLC, 47; Todd Warshaw/Getty Images, 48; Albert L. Ortega/Getty Images, 48; Keystone/Hulton Archive/Getty Images, 48; s_bukley/Shutterstock.com, 49; Matthew Stockman/Getty Images, 49; Associated Press, 49 (top);Associated Press, 51;Winslow Homer, 52; Associated Press, 53;Portland Press Herald/Getty Images, 54; PhreddieH3/File:PattsBlueberries.jpg/Wikimedia Commons, 55; Jeff chultes/ Shutterstock.com, 55; Associated Press, 55; age fotostock, 56; Associated Press, 58; Associated Press, 59; Associated Press, 60; Keystone/Hulton Archive /Getty Images, 62; Mark Wilson/Getty Images, 62; Allstar Picture Library, 62; steve estvanik/Shutterstock.com, 64; Lee Lockwood/File:CANNING SARDINES AT THE HOLMES PACKING PLANT IN EASTPORT - NARA - 550320.jpg/Wikimedia Commons, 67; Joel Arem/PhotoResearchers/Getty Images, 68; Hemis.fr, 68; imagebroker, 68 (top); Susan Pease, 69; age fotostock, 69; Alvis Upitis, 69 (bottom);Beth Perkins/Taxi/Getty Images, 70; Stockbyte/Getty Images, 71; Associated Press, 72; Arthur/File:Chapel 08.JPG/Wikimedia Commons 73; Dylan/File:Katahdin Northern Terminus Sign.JPG/Wikimedia Commons, 75; robert cicchetti/Shutterstock.com, 75.

Printed in the United States of America

MAINE
CONTENTS

A QUICK LOOK AT STATEHOOD: MARCH 15, 1820

State Tree: White Pine

The official state tree since 1945, the source of the Pine Tree State's nickname has been an important part of the state's economy for hundreds of years. The tallest, straightest white pines were perfect for supporting ships' sails and were called "mast pines."

State Bird: Chickadee

The state bird since 1927, the chickadee gets its name from its call, which sounds like "chick-a-dee-dee." The black-capped chickadee, about 5 inches (13 centimeters) long, can often be seen in wooded areas and backyards.

State Fish: Landlocked Salmon

The **landlocked** salmon is a freshwater fish that can weigh as much as 35 pounds (16 kilograms). Maine named this salmon its official fish in 1969. It is a natural resident of many of Maine's rivers, streams, and lakes.

MAINE

POPULATION: 1,328,361

State Cat: Maine Coon Cat

This longhaired cat originated in Maine, probably from breeds brought over by settlers. Larger and heavier than most other cats, it has a bushy tail that it wraps around itself to keep warm, as well as big round paws that serve as snowshoes.

State Animal: Moose

The largest member of the deer family in the world, a male moose may be as tall as 7 feet (2.1 meters) at the shoulders and weigh 1,400 pounds (635 kg). Maine made the moose its official state animal in 1979.

State Insect: Honeybee

Maine's bees pollinate the flowers on plants and trees, so the insects are important to orchards, farms, and gardens. Honeybees also make sweet honey used and sold throughout Maine. The honeybee was named the official insect in 1975.

Population Data: U.S. Bureau of the Census, 2010

The staggering beauty of its rocky coastline helps make Maine a popular destination for tourists.

1

The Pine Tree State

New England is made up of six states in the northeast: Connecticut, Maine, Massachusetts, New Hampshire, Rhode Island, and Vermont. Maine is the largest of the New England states. Its total land area is 30,843 square miles (79,883 square kilometers)—that is almost as big as all of the other five states put together. This comparatively large state, divided into sixteen counties, is home to a surprisingly small number of people, however. The state population is just above 1.3 million, which is smaller than the populations of forty other states. There are large portions of Maine with almost no human residents.

The state's landscape and climate can make it a tough place to live. The coastline is rocky and jagged. The farmland in much of Maine is poor, and the growing season is short. Thick forests cover 89 percent of the Pine Tree State—the highest percentage of any state in the nation. The winters are long and bitterly cold. However, these harsh conditions have given Maine residents, or Mainers, a reputation for being tough and independent. Many Mainers could not imagine living anywhere else. Many people from outside the state love Maine, too, and it is one of the country's most popular tourist destinations.

State Borders	
North:	Canada
South:	Atlantic Ocean
East:	Canada Atlantic Ocean
West:	New Hampshire Canada

The Coastal Lowlands

Maine can be divided into three main regions: the Coastal Lowlands, the Eastern New England Uplands, and the Great North Woods. The Coastal Lowlands cover the land that includes Maine's Atlantic coast. If you follow every twist and turn of the Maine coast, it is an amazing 3,478 miles (5,597 km), which is about as long as the California coast. This coastline is Maine's most popular tourist destination. Summer homes line the coast, from the busy sandy beaches in the south to the quieter communities close to the Canadian border. Visitors come here to enjoy the sun and sand at Old Orchard Beach and Ogunquit, eat lobster rolls and fried clams in little seaside restaurants, shop in the outlet stores of Freeport, and photograph fishing villages and lighthouses that are centuries old.

Acadia National Park dominates Mount Desert Island.

The Coastal Lowlands are not just a playground, however. The sleek pleasure boats that glide through the water off the coast pass many working fishing boats. Every day of the year, in good weather and bad, Maine's fishers are hard at work, hauling in lobsters from the offshore waters. They work year round, so even if you see a Maine lobster for sale in the winter, you know it's fresh. Maine's fishermen also bring in cod and haddock from farther out in the Gulf of Maine.

When the last Ice Age ended about ten thousand years ago, the retreating **glaciers** left behind thousands of jagged inlets in the shoreline. The glaciers also created more than two thousand islands along the Maine coast.

The most famous island in Maine is Mount Desert, home to Acadia National Park, which is the only national park in New England. Mount Desert measures 100 square miles (260 sq. km) and is covered with tall peaks, including Cadillac Mountain, which rises up to 1,530 feet (466 m) and is the highest point on the Atlantic coast of North America. The town of Bar Harbor is also located on Mount Desert. This town is a popular tourist destination as well as a thriving seashore community.

Almost half of Maine's population lives within about 20 miles (32 km) of the Atlantic Ocean. Portland, the state's largest city with more than sixty-six thousand people, is found on the Atlantic coast, on sweeping Casco Bay. Portland has been an important seaport and shipbuilding center for centuries. Today, it also has high-tech industries and an international airport.

Early Riser

The easternmost city in the United States is Eastport. It is considered the first place in the United States to receive the light of the morning sun.

The Eastern New England Uplands

Just a few miles inland is the beginning of Maine's largest region, the Eastern New England Uplands. Here, the retreating glaciers left behind gently rolling hills, hundreds of rivers, and thousands of lakes, and the best farmland in the state.

The Uplands are home to most of Maine's agriculture. The area around Augusta, the state capital, is dotted with apple orchards. In 2010, Maine produced twenty-nine million pounds (thirteen million kg) of apples. Many dairy farms dot the Uplands, home also to the blueberry barrens in the northeastern corner of the state.

Maine's most important agricultural area is Aroostook County, which Mainers call the County, along the Canadian border. In this part of the state, students are given a "harvest

MAINE
COUNTY MAP

AROOSTOOK
PISCATAQUIS
SOMERSET
PENOBSCOT
WASHINGTON
FRANKLIN
HANCOCK
WALDO
OXFORD
KENNEBEC
KNOX
ANDROSCOGGIN
LINCOLN
SAGADAHOC
CUMBERLAND
YORK

MAINE POPULATION BY COUNTY

Androscoggin County	107,702
Aroostook County	71,870
Cumberland County	281,674
Franklin County	30,768
Hancock County	54,418
Kennebec County	122,151
Knox County	39,736
Lincoln County	34,457
Oxford County	57,833
Penobscot County	153,923
Piscataquis County	17,535
Sagadahoc County	35,293
Somerset County	52,228
Waldo County	38,786
Washington County	32,856
York County	197,131

Source: U.S. Bureau of the Census 2010

A lobsterman can expect to fill his traps in the waters off Maine.

In Their Own Words

"Island living takes a special kind of person. It's an hour's ride on the ferry just to get to the mainland, so you have to be able to take care of yourself. You also have to know how to get along with people, because this is such a close-knit community."

–A year round resident of the island of North Haven

break" in the fall to help with potato farming. The County takes up 6,453 square miles (16,713 sq. km), making it Maine's largest county by far. Aroostook County is bigger than Connecticut and Rhode Island put together.

Bangor, on the Penobscot River, is the heart of Maine's lumber industry. For many years, loggers floated fallen trees downriver to Bangor, where they were cut into boards for construction or mashed into pulp for paper.

The Uplands also have many industrial centers, such as the twin cities of Lewiston and Auburn. These cities face each other from opposite banks of the Androscoggin River. Lewiston is the state's

Some farmers let people pick their own lowbush blueberries.

The Penobscot named Mount Katahdin, which in their language means "the greatest mountain."

second-largest city. Another important Upland city is Bangor, on the Penobscot River. Bangor is the heart of Maine's all-important lumber industry. For many years, loggers floated fallen trees downriver to Bangor, where they were cut into boards for construction or mashed into pulp for paper.

Tourists come to the Uplands, too, to stay in little cabins, called camps, and fish, hunt, canoe, and hike. Most of Maine's more than two thousand lakes and ponds are found in the Uplands. This includes the biggest of them all, Moosehead Lake. More than three hundred islands can be found on Moosehead Lake, which is 40 miles (64 km) long.

The Great North Woods

To the north and west of the Uplands is the region that shows most clearly why Maine is called the Pine Tree State. This area, the Great North Woods, is mostly untouched by human beings. The trees grow so thick and close here that, in many places, walking is nearly impossible.

10 KEY SITES

Acadia National Park

Eartha

Fort Knox

1. Acadia National Park

This magnificent treasure of natural beauty is located mostly on Mount Desert Island, home to the famous coastal community Bar Harbor. Among its many attractions are Sand Beach, Thunder Hole, Otter Cliff, and Cadillac Mountain.

2. Bar Harbor

Bar Harbor is renowned for offering a splendid opportunity to see some of the largest and most magnificent creatures of the sea. There are a number of whaling tours that can be hired May through October for expeditions.

3. Casco Bay

This deepwater harbor surrounds Portland and features water vessels from cruise ships to ferries to lobster trawlers. A marine gateway to Freeport, home to Maine's retail institution L.L.Bean, it is also home to many iconic lighthouses and historic forts.

4. Eartha, the Revolving Globe

This revolving globe measures 41.5 feet (13 m) in diameter and is the largest image of the Earth ever created. It is located in a three-story glass **atrium** at the Delorme corporate headquarters in Yarmouth.

5. Fort Knox

Strategically located on the west bank of the Penobscot River in Prospect, the pentagon-shaped fort was established in 1844 to guard against a possible British naval incursion. It was named after Major General Henry Knox, the first United States Secretary of War.

MAINE

6. Fort Western

Built on the banks of the Kennebec River near Augusta in 1754, this is the oldest surviving wooden fort in New England. Benedict Arnold used it as a staging location for his assault on Quebec in 1775.

7. Mount Katahdin

Situated in Baxter State Park, Mount Katahdin rises over Maine's Great North Woods. It is the tallest mountain in the state at 5,268 feet (1,606 m). Its summit marks the beginning of the Appalachian Trail.

8. Portland Head Light

Commissioned by George Washington in 1791, the majestic Portland Head Light is one of sixty-five still standing lighthouses in Maine (also known as the lighthouse state) and towers more than 100 feet above Portland Harbor.

9. Portland Museum of Art

Maine's largest and oldest art institution, founded in 1882, is home to the work of American artists as diverse as Winslow Homer, Louise Nevelson, and Andrew Wyeth, and European masters including Edgar Degas and Pablo Picasso.

10. Quoddy Head State Park

The park is located on the easternmost point on the mainland of the United States in Lubec. It has 5 miles (8 km) of hiking trails, forests, bogs, forests, and a striped lighthouse that was built in 1808.

Fort Western

Portland Head Light

West Quoddy Head Lighthouse

The Longfellow Mountains run through the heart of this region. These mountains are part of the much-larger Appalachian Range. The highest of the Longfellows is Mount Katahdin. Mount Katahdin is surrounded by Baxter State Park, a favorite spot for campers and hikers, and especially for people hiking on the Appalachian Trail. This rugged trail runs for 2,174 miles (3,499 km), through fourteen states. It ends at Springer Mountain in Georgia.

The Longfellow Mountains are great for winter sports, such as downhill skiing or snowboarding on Sugarloaf Mountain, Maine's second-highest peak. Farther north in the Great North Woods, beyond the mountains, is the Allagash Wilderness Waterway. The Allagash is a 92-mile (148-km) chain of rivers and lakes that attracts canoeists and white-water kayakers from all over the world.

Climate

For six to eight months of the year, Mainers enjoy a pleasant, mild climate. Spring in Maine can be a delight. The summers are usually comfortable, too, with days that are warm but not too hot. Nighttime temperatures can drop suddenly, however, especially along the coast.

The remote Allagash River provides more than 92 miles (148 km) of canoeing on a wilderness waterway.

Snow can stay on the ground for half the year in Maine.

In autumn, the leaves of this heavily wooded state turn to glorious reds, oranges, and yellows. But a Maine autumn can also have some dangers. Nor'easters are huge, violent storms that can blow in with hurricane force from the Atlantic Ocean.

You have to be tough to make it through a Maine winter, which can seem to last forever. Winter weather conditions can last from late November to early May. The Maine coast receives about 60 inches (152 cm) of snow during an average winter. Deep in the interior of the state, the snowfall is even heavier, at about 100 inches (254 cm).

The average low temperature along the coast in January is 13 degrees Fahrenheit (–11 degrees Celsius). Inland, especially in the northern parts of the state, it is even colder. The average January low for Caribou, near the Canadian border, is 1°F (–17°C). Maine's rivers and lakes ice over.

A Long Walk

Myron Avery became the first person to walk the entire length of the Appalachian Trail in 1936. He did it in sections over the course of sixteen years. In 2011, long-distance hiker Jennifer Pharr Davis completed the fastest-ever "thru-hike" of the Appalachian Trail. It took her forty-six days, eleven hours, and twenty minutes.

10 KEY PLANTS AND ANIMALS

Atlantic Puffin

Harbor Seal

Pink Lady Slipper

1. Atlantic Puffin

These unusual-looking seabirds, with their big blue, red, and yellow beaks, almost disappeared from Maine in the 1800s. However, beginning in 1973, Project Puffin brought baby puffins to live on some of Maine's offshore islands and they are again plentiful.

2. Black Bear

The only bear living in the eastern United States, the black bear is found nearly statewide in Maine but is most common in the heavily forested areas of eastern and northern Maine.

3. Bobcat

Though rare in northwestern Maine because of the deep winter snowfalls, the Maine bobcat is common throughout the rest of the state. Reclusive and rarely observed in the wild, the bobcat has a black and white tail and distinctive tufted ears.

4. Harbor Seal

Harbor seals were once at risk of becoming endangered in Maine. From 1905 until 1962, hunters were awarded one dollar for every seal they killed. Environmental laws now help protect these migratory mammals, and today they live in almost every harbor along Maine's coast.

5. Lady Slipper

There are four members of this rare member of the orchid family in Maine, including the Pink Lady Slipper, or moccasin flower. Its pouches force a bee to move in a direction that ensures it contacts pollen to fertilize it and other flowers.

MAINE

6. Lupine

One of Maine's best-known symbols, these tall wildflowers can be found throughout the state's forests and fields. Lupines are commonly deep purple, lavender, pink, or white. Deer Isle holds a lupine festival every June, when the flowers are at their peak.

7. Lynx

Although lynx are similar in size and appearance to the bobcat, they appear larger because of their much longer legs. The most distinguishing characteristic of the lynx is its unusually large, densely furred feet that help it travel over snow.

8. Maine Wild Blueberries

Growing wild over 60,000 acres (24,281 ha) from Maine's Downeast coast to its southwest corner, Maine's wild blueberries continue to be an important part of Maine's agricultural history. Also known as lowland blueberries, they are one of four fruit crops native to North America.

9. Moose

Moose are enormous herbivores (plant eating) whose males can grow up to 7 feet (2.1 m) tall and weigh more than 1,000 pounds (453 kg). Male antlers can span more than 5 feet (1.5 m) and weigh more than 40 pounds (18 kg).

10. Snowshoe Hare

Larger than the New England rabbit, the snowshoe hare is found throughout Maine. Its fur turns white in the winter. It can thrive in the snow-covered northern and western parts of the state in the winter months.

Lupine

Moose and her Calf

Snowshoe Hare

Wildlife

About half of Maine is **uninhabited**, which helps make the state ideal for wildlife. The skies above the coast are filled with hundreds of species of birds, from bald eagles and ospreys to cormorants and puffins. The ocean waters are home to several kinds of seals, lobsters, crabs, clams, mussels, scallops, shrimp, and sea urchins. The many species of fish include cod, flounder, and mackerel. A little farther out in the ocean, it is not unusual to see porpoises and whales breaking the surface.

The mainland is home to a wonderful variety of wildlife—especially in the North Woods. Here, black bears search for mountain cranberries, while moose nibble on water plants, and white-tailed deer shelter their young. There are also beavers, porcupines, snowshoe hares, and bobcats.

Whale watching tours are available in many towns along Maine's coastline.

The golden eagle is one of the hardest birds to spot in Maine.

This heavily forested state is covered with balsam, beech, birch, maple, oak, and of course, pine trees. In the spring and summer, many parts of Maine are carpeted with wildflowers, including the black-eyed Susan, the lady slipper, and a favorite of Mainers, the tall, colorful lupine.

The people of Maine live very close to nature, so they care deeply about preserving their natural environment. Mainers have created many laws and regulations to protect the land and wildlife of their state. However, many of Maine's species—from the golden eagle to the box turtle—are endangered (in danger of becoming extinct or completely dying out). Continuing efforts to protect the environment and Maine wildlife will help save the state's endangered species.

The Abbe Museum in Bar Harbor celebrates Wabanaki culture and history.

2

From the Beginning

People have lived in this region for thousands of years. Very little is known about the first of these early Native Americans, who are called Paleo-Native Americans. They probably hunted caribou and other large animals by using stone weapons. **Archaeologists** have found stone tools dating back to around this time.

A new group of Native Americans appeared around 2500 BCE. They are known as the Red Paint People because they buried their dead in elaborate graves colored with red pigment. They seem to have disappeared by about 1800 BCE. Centuries later, probably around 700 CE, another group of Native Americans lived along the coast. These people were probably fishers. They are known as "ceramic people" because of the clay vessels they left behind.

Explorers and Settlers

Historians debate which Europeans were the first to visit Maine. Some believe it was the Vikings, who were warriors originally from Norway and Denmark. After reaching Greenland, they sailed their longships down the east coast of North America, perhaps as early as 1000 CE.

John Cabot wearing traditional Venetian clothing, in a 1762 painting by Giustino Menescardi.

Beginning in the 1500s or shortly before, other European explorers began visiting what is now Maine. Giovanni Caboto (also known as John Cabot), an Italian sea captain who sailed for England, may have traveled along the coast in 1497. Historians have never been able to agree on his landing site. In 1524, another Italian explorer, Giovanni da Verrazzano, landed at Casco Bay, near present-day Portland. Because his ship was owned by France, he claimed the land for the French. Early European visitors described Maine as beautiful but dangerous. Tension between Verrazano and the Abenaki led to his calling the region "the Land of Bad People."

The first European attempt to settle in present-day Maine ended in disaster. In 1604, Pierre du Guast—part of a French expedition led by the explorer Samuel de Champlain—built a small outpost on an island at the mouth of the Saint Croix River. The French called the island Île des Monts Déserts. Today, it is known as Mount Desert Island. Champlain went up the Penobscot River, as far as where Bangor is today. When he returned the following spring, he found more than half of Guast's crew dead or dying, most from a disease called **scurvy**, which is caused by a diet lacking in vitamin C. The outpost was abandoned.

The French never again tried to settle in Maine. Instead, they traded extensively with the Abenaki for animal furs to sell in Europe. The French became the Abenaki's most important trading partners and closest allies. This would later cause great problems with the next group to settle in Maine—the English.

A Century of War

The English were living in what is now Maine as early as 1607, when captains Raleigh Gilbert and George Popham established a colony near the mouth of the Kennebec River. The Popham Colony was established in August and hit hard by its first brutal winter. Many of the colonists died, including Popham. In 1608, Gilbert and the remaining colonists sailed back to England.

In 1622, the English king, James I, granted a large piece of land in New England to two English nobles, Sir Ferdinando Gorges and John Mason. Seven years later, the two men split up the land, with Gorges taking the northern section, which was the part that became Maine. Mason's share is now New Hampshire. In 1652, the small, scattered English settlements of Maine came under the control of the older, more established Massachusetts Bay Colony.

Maine's first European settlement was near this shoreline in Popham Beach State Park.

The Native People

The Abenaki, or "people of the dawn," had joined other tribes living in what is now Maine by the time the European settlers arrived, including the Penobscot, the Passamaquoddy, and the Maliseet. The Abenaki are part of the much larger Algonquian group, which includes tribes that lived throughout New England and other areas of northern North America.

Among these four tribes, the men were hunters, going for big game such as deer and moose, expert fishermen and were, at times, also warriors. The women farmed the land, cared for the children, and did most of the cooking. They lived in birch-bark covered wigwams shaped more like cones than the rounded domes build by Native Americans to the south. Both men and women participated in storytelling, arts and crafts, music and traditional medicine. The men made canoes out of birch bark and fished from them using either pronged spears or harpoons.

For centuries, the Abenaki fought their traditional enemies, the Iroquois, who lived to the north and the west of them. By the 1600s, war had weakened the Abenaki, making it difficult for them to face a new threat—the arrival of the Europeans and their deadly diseases. By the 1700s, the Micmac had moved down from Canada, and they joined the four existing tribes in forming what is called the Wabenaki Confederacy.

The region's Native Americans lived in wigwams covered in birch bark.

There are five federally recognized tribes in the state today. They are the Aroostook Band of Micmacs, the Houlton Band of Maliseet Indians, the Passamaquoddy Tribe of Indian Township, the Passamaquoddy Tribe at Pleasant Point, and the Penobscot Nation. Many Penobscot live on the tribal reservation near Old Town. The tribe supported the Patriots in the American Revolutionary War. In 1980, it was awarded more than $80 million by Congress as reparations for the taking of lands from the tribe in the eighteenth and nineteenth centuries. The tribe has its own autonomous government and has one representative in the Maine Legislature who serves without a vote. The Abenaki, who had been heavily missionized by the French Jesuits, sided with France in wars against Britain. Today, there are no Abenaki reservations in the United States.

Spotlight On the Penobscot

Organization: The Penobscot are the largest group of Native Americans living in Maine. Penobscot means "the place where the rocks open out." The Penobscot did not live in traditional tents or tepees, but rather small birch bark houses called wigwams. The Penobscot formed villages where they lived in a community most of the year. However, in winter the Penobscot families would retreat to their traditional hunting grounds to seek game. In the springtime, the dispersed families would reconvene at the villages.

Clothing: Penobscot men wore breechcloths with leggings. A breechcloth is a piece of cloth, animal fir, or tanned deerskin that is worn between the legs. It is tucked into a belt in the front and back so the cloth hangs down. The leggings are tubes that give each leg protection and they are tied to the same belt. The women wore long dresses with removable sleeves. Penobscots also wore cloaks with pointed hoods, moccasins, and nose rings.

Art: Penobscot artists are best known for their quilt work, beadwork, and basket weaving. Like other Native American tribes, Penobscots also made wampum from white and purple shells.

Roles: In the past, only men could be a chief, but that changed and today a woman can also be a chief. The men would fish the Penobscot River and track and hunt moose, deer, and other game. Penobscot women farmed a variety of vegetables and starch including corn, beans, and berries, and they tapped maple trees to make syrup, much as we do today.

The English soon came into conflict with the French, who also wanted to control Maine and its rich resources. In 1689, the English began fighting the first of a long series of wars against the French and their Abenaki allies. These conflicts, sometimes known as the Colonial Wars, lasted almost a century.

Life was hard for the early European settlers of Maine, but it was far harder for the Native Americans. Europeans brought diseases to which the native population had no resistance. From 1616 to 1619, disease wiped out a large portion of their population. This time period is now known as the "Great Dying." Later, many Abenaki fled the French-English fighting to live in French-controlled areas in Canada.

Exclusive Neighborhood

Acadians were descendants of French settlers who populated what was called Acadia, which covered parts what is now coastal Canada and into Maine. The British expelled approximately 11,500 Acadians from the region starting in 1755. Many settled in Louisiana and established the Cajun culture.

The last of the Colonial Wars was the French and Indian War, between France and its Native American allies, including the Abenaki, and Great Britain and its **indigenous** allies. Many Abenaki were killed in this conflict, which was won by the British. As a result, the French signed an agreement that gave Britain control of virtually all the land France had claimed in eastern North America.

By the time the French and Indian War came to an end, thousands of British colonists were living in Maine. Settlers were moving farther inland, clearing the forests to create farmland. There was a period of peace in Maine, but it did not last long.

More Wars

By the 1770s, many people in Britain's American colonies were ready to be free of British rule. The colonists had to pay taxes on many items, including tea, but they felt they had no voice in their government. Opposition to British rule led to the American Revolution (1775–1783).

One British law that Mainers hated was the mast preservation law. According to this law, the area's largest white pines belonged to the king—to be used as masts for British navy ships. Government-appointed "mast agents" marked the trees that the colonists were not permitted to cut down.

Mainers played an important role before and during the war. They burned British tea shipments in York in 1774, in an incident known as the York Tea Party. When the American Revolution started in 1775, the people of Maine fought hard on the side of independence. The first naval battle of the war was in June 1775, around the port of Machias, when Mainers seized a British ship called the *Margaretta*. The Mainers used their knowledge of the land to their advantage. They sometimes extinguished the signals in the lighthouses along the coast, which caused British ships to run onto the rocks.

Maine paid a high price for its actions against the British. In October 1775, the British attacked the city of Falmouth, now Portland, to punish the colonists for their acts of rebellion. In what is now called the Burning of Falmouth, hundreds of buildings were burned to the ground, and most of the ships in the harbor were sunk. When the war ended in 1783—with an American victory and independence—Maine worked hard to recover. Falmouth was rebuilt. Maine's shipyards hummed with activity, as timber from the state's pine forests was used to make wooden sailing ships.

Many new settlers arrived in Maine. Huge pieces of land—totaling about 12.5 million acres (5 million hectares)—were taken from the Passamaquoddy and Penobscot and given to soldiers who had fought in the American Revolution. For a time, the region was

More than four hundred buildings were razed in the burning of Falmouth in 1775.

Making An Egg Carton Lobster

What do most people think of when someone mentions Maine? Lobster! You can make your own crustacean out of milk cartons.

What You Need

Egg carton that held 10 or 12 eggs

Three red pipe cleaners

Red paint

A hole punch

Scissors or a craft knife

Glue

A kitchen skewer (for small holes)

Two small googly craft eyes

What to Do

- To make the body of your lobster, trim down four cups of the egg carton in a row so they have rounded edges. One cup is the head, the other three are the body.
- Cut two more cups from the carton to make a tail and two claws.
- Paint all of the egg carton pieces red.
- Cut one of the egg cups in half and trim the two halves so they resemble claws. Cut the remaining cup in half and trim it to make a tail.
- Punch one hole in each side of each cup of the lobster's body. Punch two holes in its "head" to thread the arm claws through.
- Trim your pipe cleaners to a good leg length and thread three of those through the leg holes in the body.
- Now, thread a pipe cleaner through the front head part.
- Attach the claws by piercing a small hole in each one with a skewer. Push the pipe cleaner through, and bend it to keep it in place.
- Glue the tail on to the end of your lobster's body.
- Now for some eyes: You'll need two short pieces of pipe cleaner—about 1.18 inches (3 cm) each. Use your skewer to pierce two holes into the top of his head. Push the pipe cleaner through, with one end left to stick up about 1 inch (2.5 cm). Turn the lobster over and bend the ends of the pipe cleaners to hold it in place underneath.
- Glue two googly craft eyes to his antennas.

That's it. You've made a Maine lobster!

prosperous and peaceful. However, Maine's good times were eventually shattered by war. Mainers were almost as unhappy with the state government in Massachusetts as they had been with their British rulers. This turned into great bitterness during a conflict between Britain and the new United States called the War of 1812.

The British took control of a long stretch of the northern Maine coast, from Belfast to Eastport, close to the Canadian border. They cut off all contact with the outside world, and the Maine economy suffered terribly. Maine asked Massachusetts for help—but no help came. The War of 1812 officially ended in 1814.

Statehood

After the War of 1812, the people of Maine demanded statehood. They got their wish on March 15, 1820. Maine became the twenty-third state in the United States. Portland was named its capital. In 1832, the capital was moved to Augusta.

Trees have been harvested in Maine for shipbuilding, construction, and making pulp and paper.

Maine's statehood in 1820 came as part of an agreement in the U.S. Congress that became known as the Missouri Compromise. At the time, there were eleven free states (states that did not allow slavery) and eleven slave states in the young country. The Missouri Compromise called for Maine to enter the Union (another name commonly used for the United States at the time) as a free state and Missouri as a slave state. With this compromise, the numbers of free and slave states remained equal and helped balance power between the North and the South. Ships from all over the world filled Maine's harbors, their **cargo** holds waiting to carry away the state's products: fish, timber, and stone. They even carried blocks of ice—cut from frozen rivers and packed in sawdust to keep from melting—to keep food cold in the days before refrigerators.

In 1839, the United States and Britain almost went to war yet again. This time, it was over the boundary between northern Maine and British-owned Canada. The Treaty of Paris, the peace agreement that ended the American Revolution in 1783, had not clearly defined the boundary of this timber-rich region. A treaty ended the so-called Aroostook War, which never actually escalated into a military conflict, in 1842.

By the mid-1800s, mill towns were springing up all over the Maine Uplands. The rushing waters of the Androscoggin and other rivers powered sawmills, **textile** mills, and shoe factories. The mills employed immigrants, who were beginning to arrive in Maine in large numbers for the first time. Many of these immigrants came from Canada.

The Civil War

In the 1850s, Americans remained divided over the issue of slavery. Many states, especially in the South, allowed whites to own African Americans as slaves. But many New Englanders did not agree with this practice. The fight against slavery became an important cause for millions of Americans.

Some people believe one of the turning points in the debate over slavery came when a woman in Brunswick, Maine, sat down to write a book. Her name was Harriet Beecher Stowe, and the book, published in 1852, was Uncle Tom's Cabin. This novel described the mistreatment of Southern **plantation** slaves and their attempts to escape to the free states in the North. Many publishers were reluctant to publish such a controversial tale. Only five thousand copies of the first edition were printed. The books sold out in two days. By the end of the year, Uncle Tom's Cabin had sold more than 300,000 copies. The novel helped open many people's eyes to the evils of slavery.

In 1861, when the North and South could not resolve their differences, they went to war. The Civil War (1861–1865) cost nearly 400,000 Americans their lives.

An estimated seventy thousand Mainers fought on the Northern, or Union, side. At the Battle of Gettysburg in 1863, the Twentieth Maine Regiment, outnumbered two to one by the Southern forces, fought until they ran out of ammunition. Then, at the order of Colonial Joshua Chamberlain, they charged with bayonets, forcing the Southerners to retreat. Chamberlain, a former Bowdoin College professor and future state governor, received the Medal of Honor for his role. This turned the tide in one of the largest and most important battles of the Civil War. Though none of its battles were fought in Maine, more than seven thousand of Maine's young men died serving in the war.

In Their Own Words

"For the brilliant success of the second day's struggle, history will give credit to the bravery and unflinching fortitude of [the Twentieth Maine] more than to any equal body of men upon the field."

–General James C. Rice, in his report on the second day of the Battle of Gettysburg

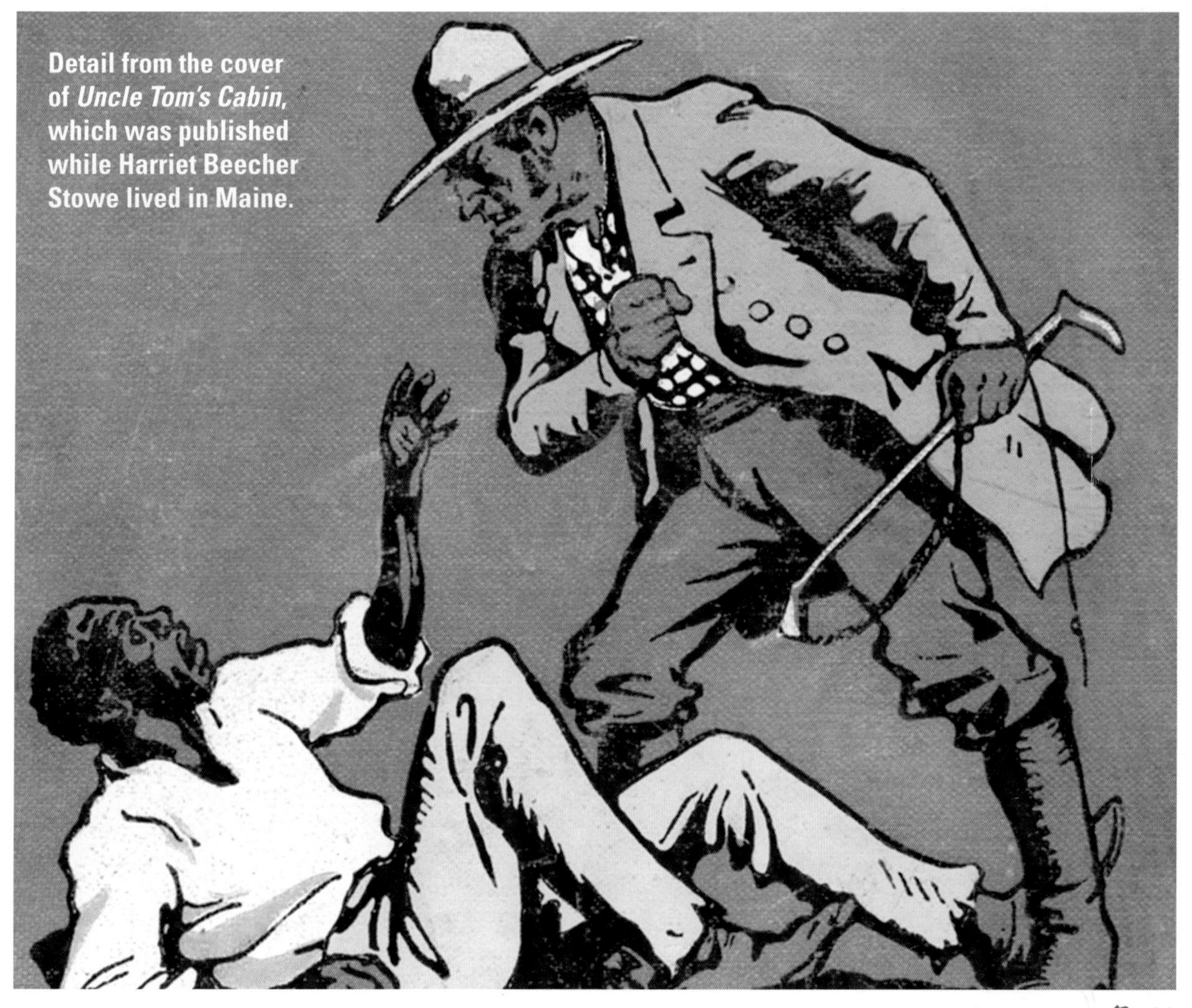

Detail from the cover of *Uncle Tom's Cabin,* which was published while Harriet Beecher Stowe lived in Maine.

10 KEY CITIES

Great Falls Balloon Festival

State Fair

Fort Preble

1. Portland: population 64,249

Portland, which sits at the mouth of the Casco Bay, is the artistic and cultural capital of Maine. The Maine Narrow Gauge Railroad provides a great view of the harbor, and it is home to all of the state's pro sports teams.

2. Lewiston: population 35,690

Home to Bates College and the annual Great Falls Balloon Festival, Lewiston is across the Androscoggin River from Auburn. The famous heavyweight championship fight between then Cassius Clay (Muhammad Ali) and Sonny Liston took place at the Colisée on May 25, 1965.

3. Bangor: population 31,473

Bangor is a major commercial and cultural center for eastern and northern Maine and has hosted the annual State Fair for more than 150 years. The University of Maine is in the town of Orono, which borders Bangor.

4. South Portland: population 23,329

South Portland is situated on the Portland Harbor, south of the Fore River. Fort Preble was built there in 1808 to protect Portland Harbor. South Portland is a thriving center for retail and industry in the region.

5. Auburn: population 23,203

Auburn is often linked to Lewiston, and the two are often abbreviated as "L-A" or "L/A." Settled in 1786, Auburn was known in the late nineteenth century as the white canvas shoe capital of the world.

MAINE

6. Biddeford: population 22,000

Located on the southeast coast of the state, Biddeford was a thriving industrial town in the nineteenth century, boasting lumber, saw, and grain mills, and textile factories. Today it is home to the Southern Maine Medical Center and the University of New England.

7. Brunswick: population 21,170

The city is the gateway to the state's Midcoast region. Brunswick is the home of Bowdoin College and the Bowdoin College Museum of Art. In 1851, Harriet Beecher Stowe published her famous book Uncle Tom's Cabin while living in Brunswick.

8. Sanford: population 20,806

Settled in 1739 and incorporated in 1768, Sanford enjoyed a robust period of textile manufacturing in the late nineteenth and early twentieth centuries. The textile mills were widely known for their mohair plush, as well as carpets, drapes, and automobile fabrics.

9. Augusta: population 18,560

Augusta was designated the state's capital in 1827. Originally an English trading post on the Kennebec River, Augusta is now home to the majestic State House, Old Fort Western, and the Pine Tree State Arboretum.

10. Scarborough: population 16,970

This popular coastal resort is located about seven miles south of Portland. Permanently settled by the English in 1749, Scarborough is home to numerous public beaches including Scarborough State Park, Higgins Beach, and Pine Point Beach.

Southern Maine Medical Center

Bowdoin College

Pine Tree State Arboretum

The Twentieth Maine, led by Colonel Joshua Chamberlain, held off a Confederate charge at Little Round Top at the Battle of Gettysburg.

Time of Growth

The years after the war brought great changes to Maine. The age of the wooden sailing ship was coming to an end, as these vessels were replaced by metal ships powered by steam. When the demand for Maine timber decreased, Mainers adapted. The state's shipyards, especially in Bath, near the mouth of the Kennebec River, began building metal ships, and they still do today.

Maine found new uses for its trees, too. Books and newspapers were becoming more common—because more people knew how to read—and their publishers needed a steady supply of paper. Pulp and paper mills were built all across northern Maine, to crush wood into pulp and then turn it into paper. Many of these mills are still in operation.

Inventing Twins

Lewiston twins Francis Edgar Stanley and Freelan O. Stanley invented the process for photographic dry plates in the 1880s and sold the patent to the company that became Eastman Kodak. They then built the Stanley Steamer, a car that set an automotive speed record of 27.4 miles per hour (44 kmh) in 1898.

These growing industries needed more and more workers, and most of them came from other countries. Many of these immigrants came from Ireland, and they gave many places in Maine Irish names, such as Belfast. Others came from Sweden to clear farmland in Aroostook County, and from Finland to work in the stone quarries along the coast. In 1870, fifty-one Swedish immigrants built a town in Aroostook County. The colony of New Sweden expanded to create the neighboring towns of Westmanland, Stockholm, and others.

The largest group of new arrivals came from the nearby Canadian provinces of New Brunswick and Quebec. These French-speaking immigrants mostly came to work in mills and factories. For many years, the French Canadians of Maine kept themselves somewhat separate from other Mainers, living and working in petits Canadas, or "little Canadas," with their own schools, churches, and businesses.

During this time, Maine's tourist industry was beginning to grow. The town of Bar Harbor, on Mount Desert Island, was a popular destination for writers and artists. By 1870, Bar Harbor had sixteen hotels. Some had two-year waiting lists for reservations.

The wealthy poured into Bar Harbor in the 1880s when Maine became a summer destination for tourists.

Many businesses closed in Maine during the Great Depression, which began in 1929.

In the 1880s, the area became a fashionable summer resort, with huge seaside mansions. Summer residents of these Bar Harbor "cottages" included members of the Rockefeller and Vanderbilt families.

Soon, steamships and railways began to bring in less wealthy visitors. They first came to spend summers on the coast, in places such as Kennebunk and Camden. Eventually resorts began to open on Moosehead and other lakes in the interior. Maine's resorts began to be an important source of jobs for Mainers.

Modern Maine

By the beginning of the twentieth century, Maine's population had grown to about 700,000. Mainers worried about how to preserve the things that made their state special. This has been one of Maine's greatest concerns ever since.

The new century was not always easy for Maine. In 1917, when the United States entered World War I (1914–1918), Maine sent about thirty five thousand soldiers to fight in Europe. During the war, the state worked to supply the war effort. After the war, the supplies were no longer needed, causing economic hardship in the state.

It was during this period that the people of Maine first began taking steps to protect their natural environment. In 1919, the U.S. Congress created Lafayette National Park, which was later renamed Acadia National Park.

It was the first national park east of the Mississippi River. Beginning in 1931, Percival P. Baxter, a former governor, began donating thousands of acres of land around Mount Katahdin. This wilderness area became Baxter State Park.

In Their Owm Words

"Monuments decay, buildings crumble and wealth vanishes, but Katahdin in its massive grandeur will forever remain the mountain of the people of Maine. Throughout the ages it will stand as an inspiration to the men and women of the state."

–Percival P. Baxter, fifty-third governor of Maine

The Portsmouth Naval Shipyard was at the center of a dispute between Maine and New Hampshire.

In the 1920s and 1930s, Mainers were mostly concerned with economic survival. Times were hard, and they worsened during the **Great Depression**. This period of economic hardship, beginning with a stock market crash in 1929, created poverty and unemployment all over the country.

During the Depression, the federal government created a program called the Civilian Conservation Corps (CCC). The CCC was designed to provide jobs for young men during this time of unemployment and poverty. In Maine, the CCC employed about twenty thousand people building public works projects, such as hiking trails through the North Woods. These workers completed the Appalachian Trail in 1937. In 1999, Maine's legislature established a memorial to the people who served in the CCC.

In From the Cold

Chester Greenwood, who was born in Farmington in 1858, is credited with inventing earmuffs. Suffering from the cold while ice skating, he shaped wires in the form of ears and asked his grandmother to sew fur to them. He made lots of money on Greenwood's Champion Ear Protectors, one of more than one hundred patents he accumulated.

In the early 1940s, Maine's economy began to improve. In 1941, the United States had entered World War II (1939–1945), which increased demand for the state's natural resources and manufactured goods. The shipyards of the coast were working day and night, as welders and mechanics built destroyers at the Bath Iron Works and submarines at the Portsmouth Naval Shipyard.

Strange as it may sound, modern Maine had a border dispute with its only New England neighbor. For more than two centuries, New Hampshire claimed the Portsmouth Naval Shipyard, at the mouth of the Piscataqua River, as part of its land. In 2001, the U.S. Supreme Court ended the controversy by ruling that it belonged to Maine. Today, the shipyard's location is listed as Kittery, Maine.

For several decades after World War II ended, Maine's economy was strong. However, in the late 1970s, that began to change. Maine's industries faced growing competition from other parts of the country, and other parts of the world. Many factories were moved to places where costs for materials and labor were lower. Two important concerns of Mainers—making a living and protecting the environment—began to come into conflict.

Millions of logs await processing at the Great Northern Paper Company at the turn of the twentieth century.

Environmentalists long had been pushing for laws to protect Maine's land and wildlife, but many Mainers worried that these laws would cost jobs. In the 1970s, for example, the state banned **clear-cutting**, a logging method that cuts down all the trees in an area, along Maine's rivers. It was thought to be harmful to the fish, especially the landlocked salmon. When environmentalists tried to stop clear-cutting everywhere in the state in 1996, the proposal was defeated. Many people were afraid it would hurt the lumber industry—and put more Mainers out of work.

The Maine economy continues to face some tough times today. More jobs were lost in the state during the nationwide recession that began in late 2007. By April 2014, the United States had recovered 101 percent of the jobs lost during the recession. However, Maine was one of five states (including Mississippi, Alabama, New Jersey, and New Mexico) that had recovered less than half of the jobs lost. However, by July 2014 the unemployment rate had fallen to its lowest point since 2008.

Paper mills closed, putting many of Maine's residents out of work.

The town of East Millinocket, hit especially hard by the recession, got a temporary reprieve when one of its two paper mills was reopened early in the recession. That relief didn't last long as the mill was temporarily shut down for restructuring and then closed for good later that summer. That mill had employed between four thousand and five thousand people in the 1970s and 1980s. However, technology has reduced demand for paper.

Other industries, from agriculture to manufacturing, are struggling. Many Mainers are still worried about their jobs. Economic instability was cited as a reason for the state's drop in children's economic well-being. The state ranked forty-sixth nationally and last in New England in wages in 2014. Many residents are also worried about preserving the natural environment and the traditional Maine way of life. But with time and effort, Mainers will find a way to endure and progress as they have for centuries.

10 KEY DATES IN STATE HISTORY

1. August 1607

The Popham Colony, which lasted only fourteen months, is established near the mouth of the Kennebec River.

2. April 10, 1641

Georgiana (now York) becomes the first chartered English city in the New World.

3. June 11-12, 1775

The American Revolution comes to Maine, with a naval engagement in Machias in which a British schooner was captured.

4. March 15, 1820

Maine becomes the twenty-third state, with Portland as its capital. The capital was moved to Augusta in 1827.

5. August 9, 1842

The Webster Ashburton Treaty settles a long-running dispute with the English over the U.S.–Canadian border. The border was in dispute after the Treaty of Paris was signed in 1783. When officials from New Brunswick, Canada, arrested Americans in the region, the Maine militia seized the area in the Aroostook War.

6. 1851

Led by Neal Dow, Maine becomes the first state to prohibit the sale and consumption of alcohol. Dow, the wealthy mayor of Portland, led raids on places that sold liquor in 1855, setting off a bloody incident with protestors.

7. August 14, 1937

Federal government crews complete the Appalachian Trail, which took more than fifteen years to finish.

8. September 13, 1948

Margaret Chase Smith of Maine is elected to the U.S. Senate. She was the first senator to denounce colleague Joseph McCarthy's tactics in his anti-communist crusade.

9. April 2, 1980

The federal courts award the Penobscot and Passamaquoddy tribes $81.5 million for the land taken from them after the American Revolution.

10. November 6, 2012

Voters in Maine approve same-sex marriage, three years after the issue was defeated in a referendum.

Residents of British and French ancestry work to preserve their cultures in Maine.

3

The People

Maine's long history has given it strong traditions and customs. Mainers are very proud of the Pine Tree State. The hardships of life in Maine have made many of the state's communities very close-knit. People in Maine tell stories of residents plowing their neighbors' driveways during heavy snowfalls, or bringing food to the elderly during power outages. The state's harsh winters mean that neighbors—perhaps more so than in other parts of the country—come to rely on each other.

In some ways, Maine is less diverse than many other states. About 95 percent of Mainers are white. The largest single ethnic group in the state is people of British ancestry, just as it has been since the eighteenth century.

This does not mean that everybody in the Pine Tree State is the same. One of the largest ethnic groups in the state is people of French Canadian ancestry. To this day, you will hear French spoken, with a Canadian accent, on the streets of Lewiston and Biddeford. Maine's French Canadians have worked hard to preserve their traditional language and culture, and their historical ties with Canada. Some of the highlights of a summer visit to Maine are festivals that celebrate the vibrant French Canadian culture, with fiddle music, folk dancing, and food.

Leaders from the Penobscot and the Passamaquoddy represented their tribes before the legislature in 2002.

Native Americans

One ethnic group that has had a very difficult time in Maine is the Native Americans. Before Europeans came to the region, the entire population was Native American. Now, they make up less than one percent of Maine's population. Many of the Abenaki of Maine live on reservations with high unemployment and poor living conditions. However, in recent years, they have worked hard to improve the standard of living on their reservations, as well as to revive their language and their traditional crafts.

Not all of Maine's Native Americans live on reservations, of course. Many live in cities and towns all over the state. Wherever they live, these populations continue to honor their heritage through traditional celebrations and festivals held throughout Maine.

Diamond in the Rough

Louis Sockalexis was the first known Native American and first minority to play in baseball's National League. He was born in 1871 on the Penobscot reservation. During a strong first season with the Cleveland Spiders, he was subjected to racial abuse. Sockalexis began drinking heavily, which helped end his career in 1899.

New Arrivals

Despite the arrival of French Canadians and others, Maine historically had fewer immigrants than most states. This, like many things about Maine, is changing. In Portland, new arrivals from other countries are beginning to transform the city's downtown area. People from countries as far away as Yemen, Iran, Somalia, and Vietnam are bringing their own cultures and traditions to the state. They open shops, restaurants, and other businesses. A city that once consisted almost entirely of people of European ancestry is now home to people from around the world. Changes are not happening just on the seacoast. Cities and towns inland also have newcomers from other countries. Many people from other states have made Maine their home, too.

Changing Times

People sometimes say there are really two Maines. What they mean is that the seacoast is, in some ways, very different from the interior. The most important difference is in economic opportunity, with more jobs available along the coast.

A vibrant Portland is attracting immigrants from all over the world.

10 KEY PEOPLE

Ricky Craven

Kevin Eastman

John Ford

1. Ricky Craven

The Newburgh-born Ricky Craven became the fifteenth driver to win a race in each of the top three NASCAR series in 2005 when he won the Kroger 200 truck series race at Martinsville Speedway. He now works for ESPN.

2. Dorothea Dix

Born in 1802 in Hampden, Dix was an early health care pioneer and tireless advocate for the care and treatment of the physically and mentally disabled. Her work with the mentally ill in prisons showed that individuals with such illnesses could be cured.

3. Kevin Eastman

This Springvale native is a comic book artist and writer who is best known as the co-creator of the global phenomenon the Teenage Mutant Ninja Turtles. He was the publisher of *Heavy Metal* magazine before selling it in 2014.

4. John Ford

The six-time Academy Award winning director was renowned for his masterful westerns. He won Best Director for *The Grapes of Wrath* in 1940 and *How Green Was My Valley* in 1941. Born in Cape Elizabeth, Ford was raised in Portland.

5. Marsden Hartley

Marsden Hartley was a prolific poet, modernist painter, and essayist. Born in Lewiston, he painted and traveled widely before returning to Maine to live full-time in 1937. The people and the rugged geography of his home state often inspired him.

MAINE

6. Anna Kendrick

The actress and singer from Portland was nominated for a Tony Award for her role as Dinah in *High Society*. She starred in the international blockbuster *Twilight* saga, and received an Academy Award nomination for her role in 2009's *Up in the Air*.

7. Stephen King

A best-selling author of horror fiction, Portland-born Stephen King has live in Maine most of his life and set many of his stories there, including *Carrie* and *Cujo*. In 2003, he was awarded the National Book Foundation Medal for Distinguished Contribution to American Letters.

8. Victoria Rowell

Born in Portland, Rowell gained fame for her roles in television's The Young and the Restless and The Cosby Show. In 2007, she won the NAACP Outstanding Debut Author award for *The Women Who Raised Me*.

9. Joan Benoit Samuelson

One of the female great distance runners in U.S. history, Cape Elizabeth native Joan Benoit Samuelson won her first Boston Marathon in 1979. A 1984 Olympic gold medalist, she won the 1985 James E. Sullivan Award as the top amateur athlete in the United States.

10. E.B. White

E.B. White is best known for his children's books, including *Charlotte's Web* and *Stuart Little*. The coauthor of *The Elements of Style*, one of the great books on how to write, he received the Presidential Medal of Freedom in 1963.

Stephen King

Victoria Rowell

Joan Benoit Samuelson

Who Mainers Are

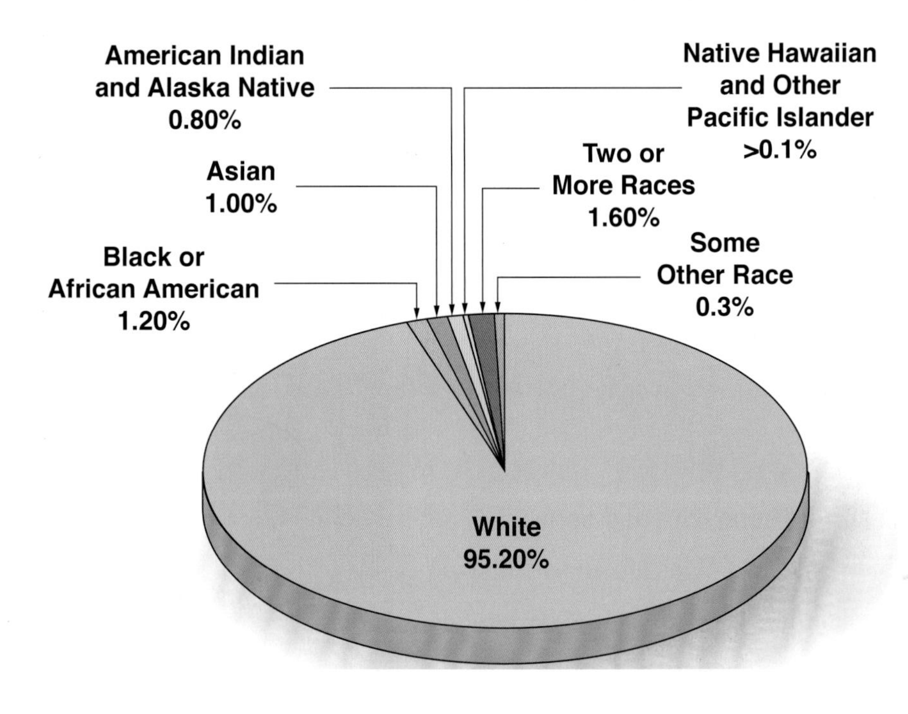

Total Population
1,328,361

Hispanic or Latino (of any race):

- **16,935 people (1.3%)**

Note: The pie chart shows the racial breakdown of the state's population based on the categories used by the U.S. Bureau of the Census. The Census Bureau reports information for Hispanics or Latinos separately, since they may be of any race. Percentages in the pie chart may not add to 100 because of rounding.

Source: U.S. Bureau of the Census, 2010 Census

The seacoast has always been more prosperous than the inland areas of the state, partially because it has more contact with the outside world. In recent years, the division between these two Maines has become even greater than in the past. Many wealthy people have moved to the seacoast, bringing more money to the region, while the resource-based industries of the interior have declined. The result is that the people who live on the seacoast have more job opportunities, and the jobs tend to pay better.

This has caused a significant change in the state's population levels. Maine's overall population had increased for hundreds of years. In some parts of northern Maine, such as Aroostook and Androscoggin counties, however, the population is now declining. Young people from these areas often have to move elsewhere to find good jobs.

Even on the seacoast, the arrival of more people, and the money they bring with them, is forcing Mainers to make difficult choices. A landowner may be tempted to sell property that has belonged to his or her family for generations, because the demand for land in some regions is so great. The pressure is especially strong along the waterfront. A small home on waterfront property may sell for millions of dollars. When these houses are sold, they are often torn down to make way for larger, more valuable summer homes.

Maine is facing one more population problem. In 2011, for the first time in seventy years deaths outnumbered births. Eleven of the state's counties experienced natural

A state education initiative put laptops in the hands of middle school students.

population decreases from July 2011 to July 2012. This trend will make it harder to find workers among an aging population.

Educational Opportunities

Some Mainers worry about educational inequality in the state. Schools in wealthier cities and towns along the seacoast can afford more learning tools, such as up-to-date computers, than schools in poorer areas of the state. One program has attempted to bring the "two Maines" together by promoting technology.

In 2002, then-governor of Maine Angus King began an ambitious project to help bridge this "digital divide." The project, the Maine Learning Technology Initiative, is a partnership with Apple Inc. that gives every middle school student his or her own personal laptop computer. At the time it was initiated, the $37.2 million contract was believed to be the largest educational technology purchase by any state. In addition to the computers, the contract included the installation of wireless Internet access in 241 middle schools, as well as technical support.

"Maine's academic standards have done a better job of integrating technology than almost every other state," said Ed Coughlin, a consultant who helped write Apple's contract proposal. "They have a level of thoughtfulness not common in most state departments of education." In 2009, this successful program was expanded to include high schools. The project shows the state's commitment to providing equal opportunities for all students.

Away from Home Rule

Eastport was held from 1814 to 1818 by British troops under King George following the War of 1812. It is the only United States owned principality that has been ruled by a foreign government.

Maine's Artists

One group of people who have never been in short supply in Maine is artists. Writers, painters, and many other kinds of artists have always been drawn to the spectacular landscapes and fascinating traditions of the Pine Tree State. Many came to Maine from elsewhere, but a large number were born in the state.

Portland's Henry Wadsworth Longfellow is a famous American poet. Other well-known Maine poets include Edna St. Vincent Millay of Rockland and Edward Arlington Robinson, who was born in Head Tide. E. B. White, author of Charlotte's Web and Stuart Little, left New York City to spend the last twenty-eight years of his life on a farm in North Brooklin. Maine's most popular living writer is Stephen King. He spends much of his year in Bangor. Maine also gave Hollywood one of its most respected directors—John Ford.

***Three Boys in a Dory* was painted by Winslow Homer, who was inspired by Maine's seascape.**

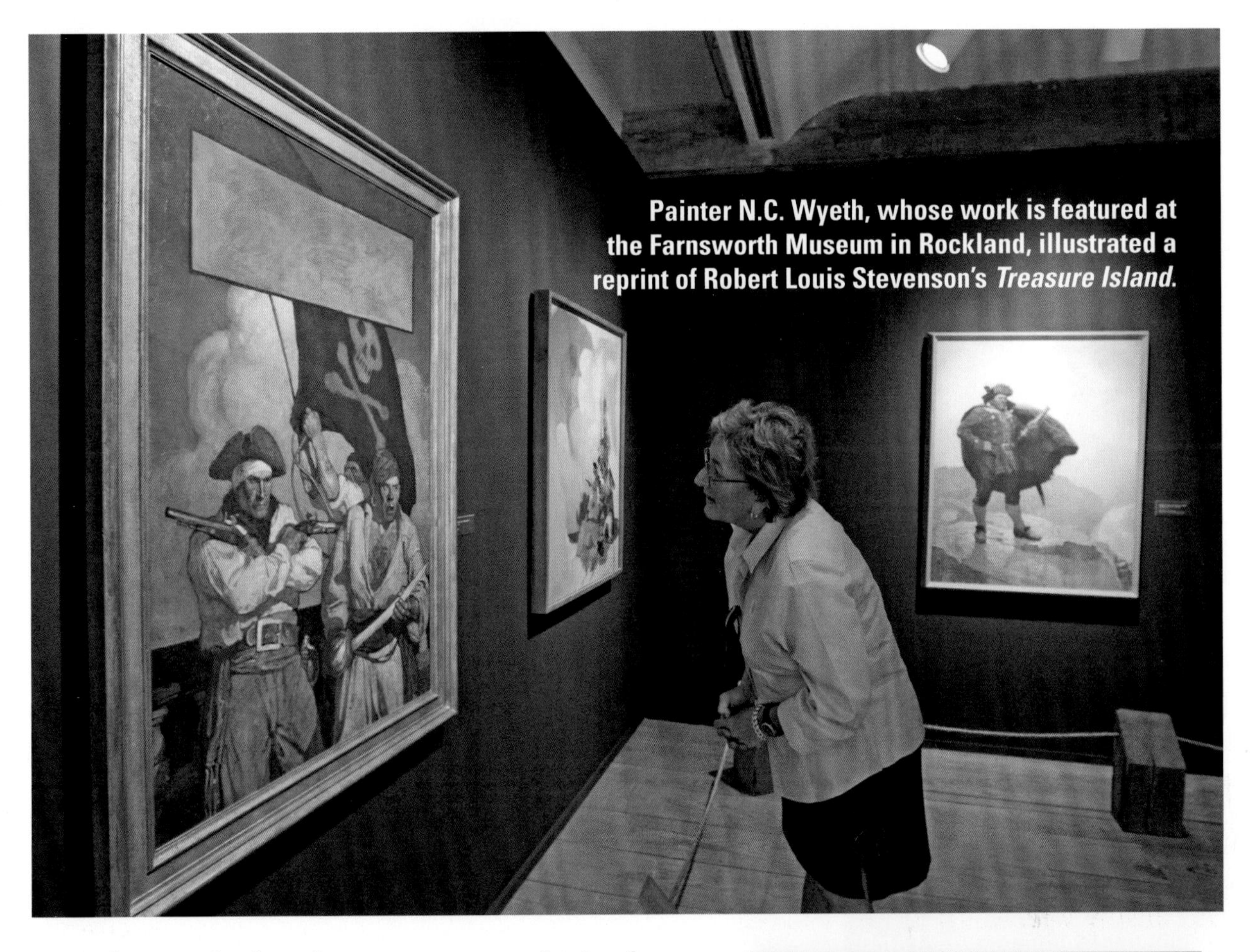

Painter N.C. Wyeth, whose work is featured at the Farnsworth Museum in Rockland, illustrated a reprint of Robert Louis Stevenson's *Treasure Island.*

He is known for his classic westerns, which often starred the legendary John Wayne.

Painters, too, have always been drawn to Maine, and especially to the breathtaking scenery of the seacoast. Winslow Homer, one of the most famous artists of nineteenth century America, spent many years depicting the state's **seascapes**. In the mid-twentieth century, Rockwell Kent became famous for his paintings of Monhegan Island, where he lived for many years. Members of the Wyeth family, including N. C., Andrew, and Jamie, have been painting in Maine for almost a hundred years.

Knocking at the Dooryard

"Dooryard" is a Maine term for the area closest to the door that is used most often, so it is usually the front yard. Walt Whitman used it in his famous poem, "When Lilacs Last in the Dooryard Bloomed," which is an elegy on the death of President Abraham Lincoln.

No matter where they are from or what they do, Mainers are proud to call the state their home. Its beautiful land, expanding cities, quality schools, charming towns, and good-hearted people all make the Pine Tree State a great place to live.

10 KEY EVENTS

Common Ground Country Fair

Maine Lobster Fest

1. Acadian Festival

The largest cultural festival in Maine happens every summer, in Madawaska, near the Canadian border. Acadian art, music, and food are featured. Every year, the highlight of the festival is a huge reunion of one of Maine's pioneering Acadian families.

2. Common Ground Country Fair

This "celebration of rural living" has been held in Unity every September since 1977. Hosted by the Maine Organic Farmers and Gardeners Association (MOFGA), the fair features food from local farms, animal exhibits, and crafts.

3. Harvestfest

Autumn is a wonderful time to visit the historic village of York, which celebrates the coming of autumn with traditional Maine crafts, wagon rides, and a corn tossing contest.

4. Machias Blueberry Festival

Held in Machias each August, this celebration of the blueberry harvest features a children's parade, fish fry, pie eating contest, and homemade blueberry pancakes. There is also live music and the Blueberry Run.

5. Maine Lobster Festival

Every August, some 100,000 lobster lovers descend on Rockland. They come to enjoy parades, music, and, of course, thousands of pounds of lobster. There is also a road race and live performances by top musical artists.

MAINE

6. Maine Maple Sunday

On the fourth Sunday in March, sugarhouses all over the state open their doors to visitors. Many houses offer demonstrations of making syrup from tree sap, as well as free samples of the sweet treat.

7. Maine Wild Blueberry Festival

The sweetest place in all of Maine may just be the little town of Union. Union celebrates the August blueberry harvest with muffins, pastries, and a pie eating contest.

8. Moose Mainea

This month-long celebration is held in Greenville each spring, and is timed to provide the best opportunities to see moose in the wild. There is a Moose River canoe race, a craft show, a Kids Day, and live entertainment.

9. National Toboggan Championships

During the first weekend in February, Camden plays host to hundreds of thrill-seeking tobogganers. The heart-stopping dash down the 400-foot (122-m) toboggan "chute" takes about ten seconds and much courage.

10. Windjammer Days

For one weekend in June, Boothbay Harbor is crowded with windjammers and other "tall ships" for a celebration of the region's maritime history. Among the events are a golf tournament, an antique boat parade, and the Annual Rocky Coast Road Race.

Maine Blueberries

National Toboggan Championships

Windjammer Days

The capitol building in Augusta was completed in 1832.

4

How the Government Works

The famous independent spirit of the Pine Tree State means the people of Maine make up their own minds. When they want something to happen, they make it happen themselves.

Two U.S. senators, who serve six-year terms in Washington, D.C., represent Maine in the federal government. The state is also represented by two members of the House of Representatives, according to the state's population as measured in the 2010 Census. The population of a state determines the number of people that it sends to the U.S. House of Representatives. Every state must have at least one member in the House. Members of the House of Representatives serve two-year terms.

The Maine **constitution**, which was adopted in 1820, divides the state government into three separate but equal branches: executive, legislative, and judicial.

The people elected to represent Maine are often every bit as independent as the people who sent them there. It is at the local level that Maine's unique brand of self-government shows most clearly. Maine has sixteen counties, twenty-two cities, and 435 towns. Under a special form of government called home rule, each local area has the right to choose its own form of local government.

Some of Maine's cities and towns have an elected mayor and a city or town council. Most of Maine's communities are run by **selectmen**, who handle the day-to-day running of the town. However, the most important decisions are made at a town meeting. Once a year, all the residents of a town can come to the annual meeting, to discuss and vote on the most important local political issues. Between meetings, an elected board supervises town decisions.

In the past, just about everybody came to the town meeting, which is usually held in March. Attendance has dropped off in recent years, however, as most town meetings are now televised live. Decisions about how to run the town and how to spend its money are made at town meetings, or voted on by secret ballot after the meeting is over. Common issues include dog leash laws, contracts for snow removal, and town budgets.

Margaret Chase Smith showed great courage as a U.S. Senator.

Residents sing the national anthem at a town meeting, where most of the local government decisions are made in Maine.

How a Bill Becomes a Law

The process of creating a new state law is a slow, careful one. A new Maine law begins as an idea that is sponsored by a member of either house of the state legislature. The member proposes the creation of a new law, and lawyers, researchers, and other legislature staff help write a draft version. This draft is called a bill.

The legislator who sponsored the bill gives it to either the clerk of the house or the secretary of the senate, depending on his or her chamber. Each bill is referred to a joint standing committee. Each of these committees considers bills by topic. If the bill is related to schools, for example, it would be referred to the joint standing committee on education and cultural affairs. The committee holds a public hearing to hear supporting and opposing arguments from the public. The committee then decides whether to suggest passing the bill as is, passing with changes (or amendments), or not passing it at all.

If the majority of the committee members support the bill, it is opened for debate within the full house or senate, with two formal readings. If the first chamber approves the bill, it goes to the other body to be considered. Both houses must agree on the exact same wording of the bill.

Tours are available in the beautiful state capitol.

Sometimes the house and senate amend bills differently. In those cases, it is sent to a conference committee. The committee will try to find a compromise. Once the state house and senate agree upon a final bill, it goes to the governor.

If the governor signs the bill, it becomes law. However, the governor may refuse to sign it. This is called a veto, and it keeps the law from taking effect. The legislature can override this veto, with a two-thirds' majority vote in both houses. If it does, the bill becomes a law even though the governor disagrees with it.

In Their Own Words

"Our future depends on government working."

–Former U.S. Senator Olympia Snowe

Branches of Government

EXECUTIVE

The executive branch, headed by the governor, makes sure that the state's laws are carried out properly and handles the day-to-day running of the state government. The governor is elected every four years, and can serve no more than two terms in a row. There is no limit on the total number of terms a governor can serve.

LEGISLATIVE

The Maine legislature is divided into two chambers: the senate and the house of representatives, which meet at the State House in Augusta. The thirty-five members of the senate and the 151 members of the house of representatives create new laws and change existing ones. They are elected by their local districts and serve for two-year terms. They can serve no more than four terms in a row.

JUDICIAL

The judicial branch settles legal disputes, punishes people who commit crimes, and decides whether Maine's laws violate the state constitution. The state's highest court, the Supreme Judicial Court, handles the most serious cases, constitutional issues, and appeals from lower courts. This court is made up of a chief justice and six associate judges. Maine's next highest court is the superior court, which handles all cases requiring a jury trial. The state also has district and probate courts. These courts handle trials without juries and civil trials involving relatively small amounts of money. All of Maine's judges are appointed by the state's governor, and serve terms of seven years. There is no limit on the number of terms they may serve.

POLITICAL FIGURES FROM MAINE

George Mitchell: U.S. Senator, 1980–1995

George Mitchell served in the U.S. Counter-Intelligence Corps and as U.S. Attorney for Maine. He was voted most respected member of the senate six straight years, and led the reauthorization of the Clean Air Act in 1990.

Edmund Muskie: U.S. Senator, 1959–1980

Edmund Muskie served one term as the governor of Maine before being elected a U.S. senator. The running mate for Hubert Humphrey's unsuccessful 1968 presidential bid, he sought the democratic nomination for president in 1972. He served as Secretary of State under President Jimmy Carter.

Olympia Snowe: U.S. Senator, 1995–2013

Born in Augusta and raised in Auburn, the republican is the first woman in to serve in both houses of a state legislature and both houses of Congress. A centrist, Snowe shockingly announced in 2012 she would not seek another term, citing gridlock.

MAINE
YOU CAN MAKE A DIFFERENCE

Contacting Lawmakers

To find contact information for Maine's state legislators, go to
www.maine.gov/portal/government/edemocracy/lookup_voter_info

Choose your city or town, and then type in your address to find your state senator and representative. You can find the leaders of your local government—the mayor, the city council members, or the selectmen—using links in the "How Do I" box to the right. There is also a Public Meeting Calendar link on this website.

Making a Difference

Kids can make a difference by participating in the law-making process. Study the legislative agenda in your state on either a local or national level and decide if there is an issue you would like to weigh in on. You can use letters or email to contact politicians.

If there is a political issue that you care about, you can make a difference. Many of Maine's laws were created because ordinary Mainers wanted them.

One example is a food sovereignty law that was passed first by Sedgwick in 2013 and had been passed by ten others as of May 2014. The ordinance was written to protect citizens' rights to "produce, sell, purchase, and consume any food of their choosing." Among these goods are raw milk and locally slaughtered meats.

The law was written to supersede any law passed by the state or federal government, including regulatory agencies. It was seen as a way to help beginning farmers and cottage producers who want to try new things without facing the burdens of government regulations.

Trees are in plentiful supply
for loggers in Maine.

5

Making a Living

Mainers have always been hardworking, because Maine can be a tough place to make a living. That has been especially true in the past few years as jobs in some parts of Maine have decreased. The northern parts of the state have been hit particularly hard. By April of 2014, the unemployment rate for all of Maine was 5.7 percent. Although that number was more than a half of a percentage point lower than the national average, in remote Washington County, in the northeastern corner of the state, the number was more than four percentage points higher.

As of 2014, Maine's economy had expanded less since 2009 than any other state except Connecticut's.

Manufacturing

Manufacturing is an important segment of the Maine economy. However, in the past few years, manufacturing industries have been badly hurt all across Maine. In the 1950s and 1960s, half of all Maine workers were employed in manufacturing, making such things as wood products, textiles, and shoes. Today, only about 9 percent of Mainers work in the manufacturing sector. That number will probably fall even lower in the years to come.

Wood products are the most important of Maine's manufactured goods. The state ships Christmas trees and wreaths, plywood, and shingles all over the world. The most important of Maine's wood products is pulp and paper. This industry, too, is suffering, with some mills closing and workers losing their jobs.

Few Neighbors

Maine is the only state that shares its border with only one other state.

One of the main reasons for this decline is foreign competition. Maine's manufacturers must now compete with products from other countries where workers' wages are lower and goods are often much cheaper to make.

Beginning in the 1990s, the shipyards of Bath and Kittery laid off many employees. This decline in the shipbuilding industry did not happen because of competition from other countries. The problem was that, in a time of peace, the U.S. military was not ordering as many ships.

From the Land and Water

It might seem surprising that Maine, with its rocky soil and short growing season, has any agriculture at all. Farming is quite important in some areas of the state, however. Farms in different parts of the state produce oats, hay, and corn. Most of these crops are used to make food for livestock. Aroostook County produces potatoes and broccoli. The Augusta area is well known for its apple farms. Other parts of Maine produce blueberries and maple syrup. Maine produces more blueberries than any other state, and it is second in the nation for maple syrup production.

Maine does not have a very large mining industry, but there are some valuable mined products. The Pine Tree State has sand, gravel, and limestone, which are used in construction. Copper and zinc can be found in northern parts of Maine, but they are not usually mined in large quantities. The state mineral, tourmaline, is mined and made into jewelry that is sold all over the world. The mineral was first discovered at Mount Mica in 1820.

Maine's fishing industry is an important part of the economy. Since the first settlements, boats and ships have gone into Maine's inland and coastal waters to catch fish and crustaceans. The fishing industry also includes the people who clean, prepare, pack, and ship the fish and crustaceans throughout the country and around the world.

Workers pack sardines at a plant in Eastport in 1973.

Lately, the stocks of ocean fish such as cod and haddock have decreased. Maine's fishing industry is regulated by a U.S. government agency called the National Marine Fisheries Service (NMFS). The agency has cut back on the numbers of fish that commercial fishers are allowed to catch. While this protects the fish populations, it has made it difficult for many of Maine's fishers to make a living. In May 2014, it was announced that Maine would receive $2.3 million out of $32.8 million set aside to help the five New England coastal states hurt by the drop in fish populations. Shrimping was shut down in the state in 2013.

The state's lobster population continues to flourish, however. In 2010, Maine's yearly lobster catch was about 93 million pounds (42 million kg). This catch, worth more than $308 million, was an increase from previous years. Other New England states have seen a decrease in the size of their lobster harvest due to rising water temperatures. So far, the coastal areas north of Cape Cod, Massachusetts, have been spared.

10 KEY INDUSTRIES

Agriculture

Fishing

Mining

1. Agriculture

Maine is the eighth-largest potato-growing state in the country. Almost 55,000 acres (22,260 ha) of Maine farmland—mostly in Aroostook County—produced more than $159 million of potatoes in 2010. Apples are the most valuable fruit crop.

2. Bottled Water

The natural springs and pristine **aquifers** of western Maine provide the source for the bottled water industry, of which Poland Spring is the most famous brand. As of early 2014, there were eighteen bottled water plants in the state.

3. Dairy Farming

At one time, Maine had more than five thousand dairy farms throughout the state. Today, however, there are only about three hundred. The products from these farms are still important to Maine. Milk and cow manure are still leading livestock products in the state.

4. Fishing

Lobster was once so plentiful in Maine that it was called "poverty food"—something even the poorest people could afford to eat. More than 80 percent of the lobsters served in the entire country come from the state, as well as other shellfish, and farm-raised Atlantic salmon.

5. Mining

Sand, gravel and limestone are the most valuable non-metallic minerals mined in Maine. Other mined products include clays, garnet, gemstones such as tourmaline [the state mineral], amethyst and topaz, granite, slate, and peat.

MAINE

6. Naval Shipbuilding

Shipbuilding has been part of the economy of the Kennebec River since 1762. The region used to build wooden ships, but now Bath Iron Works produces ships for the United States Navy. Submarines are repaired and modernized at the Portsmouth Naval Shipyard.

7. Pulp and Paper

With 89 percent of the state forested, wood products —from sailboats to paper —are an important part of the manufacturing industry. The state's mills produce approximately four million tons (3.6 million metric tons) of paper every year.

8. Shipping

The Port of Portland is New England's biggest port based on tonnage handled, and is the closest U.S. port to Europe. In addition to handling paper pulp, fish, and other food products, the port is the launching site for many passenger cruise ships.

9. Tourism

In the summer of 2010, more than twenty-three million people visited the state. People from all over the world come to experience Maine's cities, museums, historical sites, restaurants, coastal resorts, and parks.

10. Wild Blueberries

Wild lowbush blueberries—smaller and more flavorful than farm-produced highbush blueberries—grow beautifully in Maine's thin, rocky soil. In 2010, the state produced 83 million pounds (38 million kg) of blueberries.

Portland's Naval Shipyard

Tourism

Wild Blueberries

Recipe for Maine Open Blueberry Pie

This traditional Maine recipe is simple to make and delicious. You can use any kind of blueberries. If you can find lowbush blueberries from Maine—either fresh, frozen, or canned, give them a try.

What You Need

Tart pastry dough for nine inch (22.8 cm) tart
1 cup (237 milliliters) sugar
3 tablespoons (44 mL) of cornstarch
1/8 teaspoon (0.6 mL) salt
1 tablespoon (15 mL) butter
4 cups (946 mL) of fresh, canned, or thawed frozen blueberries
For whipped cream
1 cup (237 mL) heavy cream
Sugar to taste

What to Do

- Get an adult to preheat the oven to 425°F (218°C).
- Line a nine inch (22.8 cm) pie pan with the pastry dough, prick the dough all over, and bake 10–15 minutes, until lightly browned.
- Mix the sugar, cornstarch, salt and one cup (237 mL) water in a pan. Cook over low heat stirring constantly until thickened.
- Add the butter, stir until melted, and let cool. Fold in the blueberries and pile into the baked pie shell.
- Before serving, whip the cream, adding sugar to taste, and spread it over the blueberry filling. Serve and watch people smile.

The Penobscot River provides opportunities for whitewater rafting.

Services and Tourism

The service industry includes any jobs that provide a service to others. Teachers, doctors, tour guides, waiters, and hotel clerks are all part of the service industry. The service industry employs a large number of Mainers.

Tourism is one of the most profitable parts of Maine's service industry. The Pine Tree State has something for just about every visitor. This includes the spectacular beauty of the seacoast, the unspoiled wilderness in the interior—including 436,064 square miles (1,129,401 sq. km) of national and state parks—and the peaceful, easygoing Maine way of life.

But part of what brings tourists to Maine is the people. Mainers offer visitors a friendly "down east" welcome that keeps them coming back, year after year. And that makes tourism one Maine industry that keeps growing, no matter how troubled the economy might be.

New Ways

Maine still relies heavily on its traditional industries and natural resources, such as wood and fish. It is working hard to develop modern, advanced industries, however. Financial services have become an important part of the Maine economy, as banks and insurance companies have moved their headquarters into the state. More and more technology industries, such as software companies, are moving into Maine, especially around Portland.

The University of Maine system includes the University of Southern Maine, which has its main campus at Gorham.

Bates College is one of many prestigious private colleges in the state.

Businesses are choosing to come to Maine for many reasons. The state has a fairly low cost of living, with inexpensive places to live. Traveling to and from Maine is easy, thanks to its two international airports and frequent trains and buses to Boston and New York City. Another bonus for industries and employers is the well-educated, highly skilled workforce.

Maine's workforce is often educated at the state's excellent colleges and universities. The University of Maine System (UMS) is made up of seven universities, including its flagship school, the University of Maine in Orono. More than 11,000 students attend UMaine Orono, which was founded in 1862. Maine is also known for such prestigious private colleges as Bates, Bowdoin, and Colby.

People have always had to work hard to get by in Maine, often taking on more than one job. A fisher would work as a carpenter in the winter, when it was too cold to go out on the water. A farmer might have a job in town to help make ends meet. It is this spirit—hardworking, independent, and resourceful—that has always carried Mainers through good times and bad. And it is this spirit that makes the people of Maine by far the state's most important natural resource.

MAINE STATE MAP

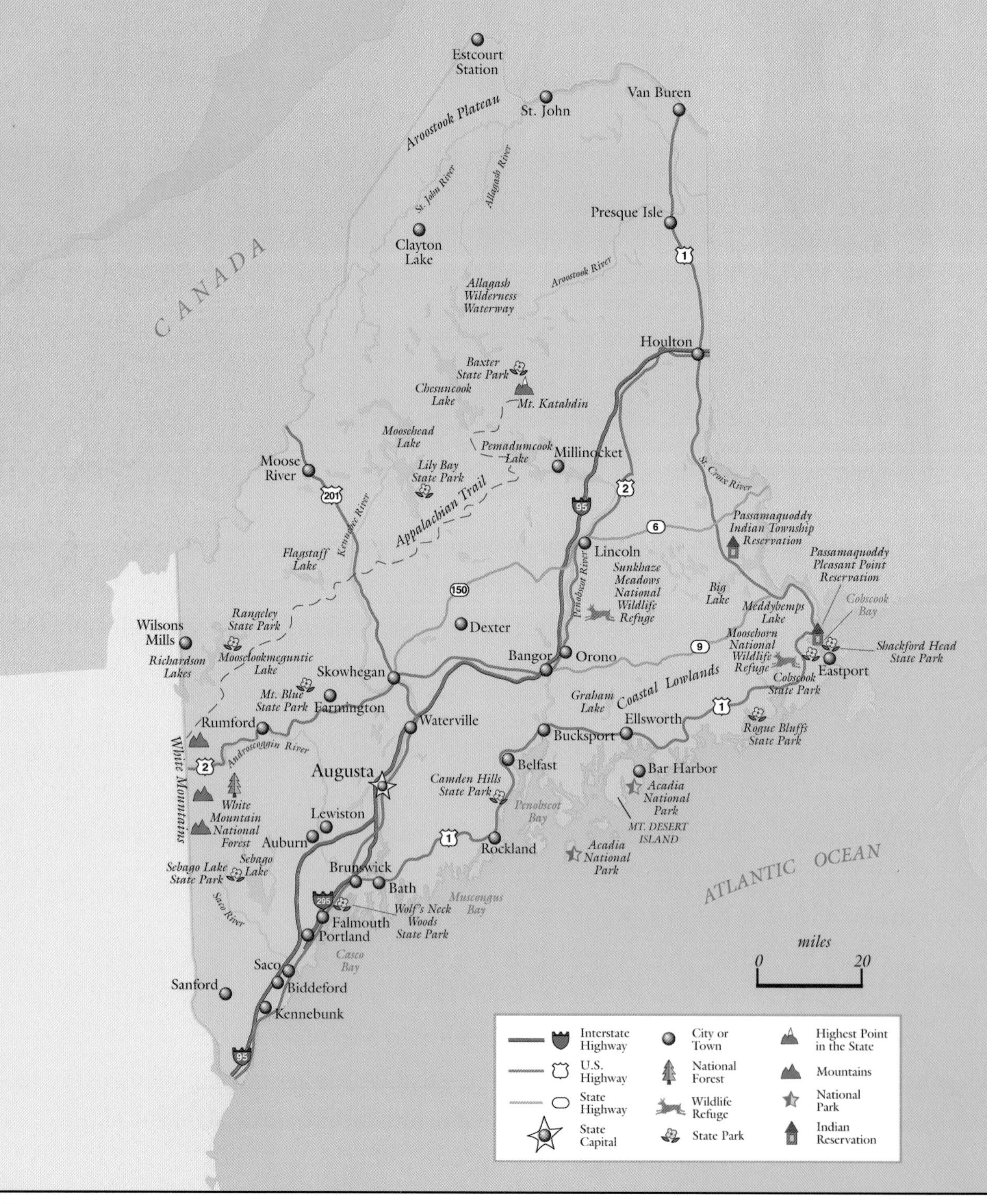

MAINE
MAP SKILLS

1. **Where does the Appalachian Trail begin in Maine?**
2. **On which highway is Moose River located?**
3. **What interstate highway begins in Maine?**
4. **Which state park is closest to the White Mountains National Forest?**
5. **What is the capital of Maine?**
6. **Lincoln is located on which river?**
7. **Which national park is located on an island?**
8. **What Maine city is closest to Orono?**
9. **What is the northernmost town in Maine?**
10. **Which National Wildlife Refuge is in the easternmost region of Maine?**

Start of the Appalachian Trail.

Moosehorn National Wildlife Refuge.

1. Mount Katahdin
2. U.S. Highway 201
3. Interstate 95
4. Sebago Lake State Park
5. Augusta
6. Penobscot River
7. Acadia National Park
8. Bangor
9. Estcourt Station
10. Moosehorn National Wildlife Refuge

State Flag, Seal, and Song

The Maine state flag, chosen in 1909, shows the state seal, against a blue background. The background is the same shade of blue as in the flag of the United States.

The state seal shows some of the people and resources that have been important throughout Maine's history. A farmer and a sailor stand on either side of a shield showing a pine tree and a moose. Above the shield is the state's motto, Dirigo, which means "I lead." Below is the word "Maine."

The state song is appropriately named "State of Maine Song." It was adopted in 1939. Roger Vinton Snow, who was a lawyer, wrote the words and music. To see the lyrics and to listen to the song, visit: **www.maine.gov/sos/kids/about/symbols/song.htm**

Glossary

aquifer A geologic formation what holds or conveys fresh groundwater.

archaeologist A person who studies ancient peoples and cultures through their artifacts.

atrium An open area inside a tall building that has windows to let light in from above.

cargo The goods carried on a ship, plane or motor vehicle.

clear-cutting To cut down or remove every tree from an area.

constitution The system of beliefs and laws by which an organization or a state governs itself.

glaciers A slowly moving mass or river of ice.

Great Depression The worldwide economic collapse following the stock market crash of 1929. Marked by very high unemployment, it lasted through much of the 1930s.

indigenous Originating naturally in a particular place.

landlocked Surrounded by land with no coastline or seaport; a lake with no route to the sea.

plantation An estate on which crops are planted and raised by resident labor.

scurvy A disease caused by a deficiency of vitamin C, characterized by swollen bleeding gums and the opening of previously healed wounds. It affected many poorly nourished sailors until the end of the eighteenth century.

seascapes A view or an artistic rendition of an expanse of sea.

selectmen A member of a local government board of a New England town.

textile A type of cloth or woven fabric.

uninhabited A place with no human residents.

More About Maine

BOOKS

D'Entremont, Jeremy. *Great Shipwrecks Off the Maine Coast*. Beverly, MA: Commonwealth Editions, 2010.

Griffin, Nancy. *Maine 101: Everything You Wanted to Know About Maine and Were Going to Ask Anyway*. Lunenburg, Nova Scotia: McIntyre Purcell Publishing, Inc. 2013.

House, Katherine L. *Lighthouses for Kids: History, Science, and Lore with 21 Activities* Chicago, IL: Chicago Review Press, 2008.

WEBSITES

Maine Historical Society:
www.mainehistory.org

Maine Office of Tourism:
www.visitmaine.com

Secretary of State's Kids' Page:
www.state.me.us/sos/kids

ABOUT THE AUTHORS

Terry Allan Hicks has written several books for Cavendish Square, including those about the states of New Hampshire and Nevada.

Amanda Hudson is a writer and editor who grew up in the small town of Readfield, Maine.

Van Kirk McCombs is a retired lawyer who lives in Jacksonville, Florida, with his family.

Index

Page numbers in **boldface** are illustrations.

Index